COPY NO. 2

D1760500

WITHDRAWN FROM THE POETRY LIBRARY

JEAN O'BRIEN
Merman

POETRY LIBRARY
SOUTHBANK CENTRE
ROYAL FESTIVAL HALL
LONDON SE1 8XX

salmonpoetry

Published in 2012 by
Salmon Poetry
Cliffs of Moher, County Clare, Ireland
Website: www.salmonpoetry.com
Email: info@salmonpoetry.com

Copyright © Jean O'Brien, 2012

ISBN 978-1-908836-03-8

All rights reserved. No part of this publication may be reproduced or transmitted in any form or by any means, electronic or mechanical, including photography, recording, or any information storage or retrieval system, without permission in writing from the publisher. The book is sold subject to the condition that it shall not, by way of trade or otherwise, be lent, resold or otherwise circulated without the publisher's prior consent in any form of binding or cover other than that in which it is published and without a similar condition, including this condition, being imposed on the subsequent purchaser.

COVER ILLUSTRATION: *Ray Murphy*
COVER DESIGN: *Siobhán Hutson*

Salmon Poetry receives financial support from The Arts Council

This book is dedicated to my siblings

'What would the world be, once bereft
of wet and of wildness? Let them be left,
O let them be left, wildness and wet;
Long live the weeds and the wildness yet.'

Inversnaid, GERARD MANLEY HOPKINS

Acknowledgements

Thanks to the editors of the following publications in which some of the poems in this collection were previously published:

"All That Jazz" was first published in *The Shadow Keeper* (Salmon, 1997). "Dear Diary" was first published in *Dangerous Dresses* (Bradshaw Books, 2005.) "Shadow" was first published in *Lovely Legs* (Salmon, 2009).

"Merman" won the 2010 Arvon (Biennial) International Poetry Competition.

Thanks to the editors of the following magazine where these poems or versions of them first appeared:
Agenda (UK), *Orbis* (Featured Poet) (UK), *New Hibernia Review* (Featured Poet) (USA), *Houston Literary Review* (USA), *Prairie Schooner* (USA), *Dunes Review* (USA), *Poetry Ireland Review, The Stinging Fly, Outburst Poetry* (ezine), *Shine On* Anthology (Dedalus Press, 2011), *Stoney Thursday*, *Windows Anthology*, *The sHOP* and *The Moth.*

"Watching for The Comet", "Sanctuary", "Keeping Shtum" and "Miss Carr's Junior School Rathgar" were first broadcast on Sunday Miscellany RTE Radio 1.

Thanks to Offaly County Council for awarding me a stay in the Tyrone Guthrie Centre, in Annaghmakerrig and to the Arts Council of Ireland for awarding me a Travel and Training grant to the USA.

Many thanks to the artist Ray Murphy for the use of a version of his print 'Merman' for the cover of this book.

Contents

Merman

I had been working in the fish farm for weeks,
that one near the river outlet and the sea.
I didn't like the work we were constantly
wet, dirty, didn't like the men there either.
They were insolent, often dropped small fry
and crushed them underfoot. One in particular
Glaucus, tall, muscular cast his sea-green eyes over me,
tried to lure me as I tipped phosphorus feed
into the holding pens that smoked and stank
and made mist veils I tried to hide within.

One day he walked towards the tanks
waders held in his large hands, he was chewing
on a herb he said was magical, always urging
me to eat it. I would not bite. Anyway whatever way
it was, he leaned to pull the waders on, both legs
got caught in one boot and over he flipped.
I cast around for help, no-one was there. I went back.
He was emerging from amongst the shoals
of salmon, clinging to his single wader
up to his waist were the glittering scales of smolts.

He rose shaking, coloured sequins waterfalling
as he tried to right himself and beckoned me for help.
I took the bait and when I caught him,
we stumbled, he landed me and pinned me down,
I looked, held his eyes, it was early the rising sun
was flooding them with hooks of golden light. I said No.
He parted my thighs and when it was over,
untangled his legs, shook the silver armour
from himself, his eyes had lost their lustre.

I left distraught and walked all day stumbling
over ditches and hillocks, stopped now and then
to eat, following the river to its source.
At so many hundred feet I rested where the stream
welled from the earth, cooled my toes, kicked gravel
into little pools and felt the flow snagging
in the waters of my womb. I cried and screamed
and shook my fists at the sky, knew then this birthing
pool was to be my fate, tried to obliterate
his sea-green eyes, his face, his terrible merman tail.

Left Over Christmas Trees

Paper never refuses ink,
no matter how hard the words
it just absorbs. In the same way
the eye never refuses the blue
of sky, the fish water, the bird
never spurns air.

In the wind leaves of eucalyptus
show their silver undersides,
you can predict rainbow weather
by the way light flattens itself
and turns chrome, or like
metal filings and lake-water it looks
dense and eloquent like mercury.

Against the bow of colours
birds are tossed about and luff off
into a wreath of gathering darkness.
Passing a forest in January
left over Christmas trees
stand rootless, bound tight
in shrouds of white netting,
swaddled in failing light
they look sinister, grey people emerging,
the sequence of time slipping.
I drove on – my wheels welcoming
the tarmac and the journey home.

Snow Ciphers

Ice crystals growing on threadbare trees
are strange fruits of rime. Cold sun brings beauty
to a cruel landscape, white has homogenised
roads and fields. Only the steaming black
or brown coats of horses stand out in relief
in this featureless backdrop.

Lambs hurtle like tossed snowballs
their mothers' lost in the need to make milk.
Birds rustle and break from every hedgerow.
I gingerly inch past robins, finches,
blackbirds – even that tiny troglodyte the wren,
all fluffed feathers, like a dust-devil bowling along.

Mostly we stay cooped up, locked in
only braving the chill to chip away
at frozen coal, its burnished black stark
against the almost monotonous white.
Fog and grey skies menace and hang heavy,
strange footprints ripen in the dark.

Visible Light

In this place the killing of birds is taboo,
the moon in a passion waxes to her full light.
The blue of sea with a pitiless sun in the sky
is like your eyes, azure, trembling,
unsure as a painter spreading colour on canvas.
You lose yourself in increments
as scales of your skin slough off
and blow away while your hands adopt
the Japanese mudra position of contemplation.

You are whiting out like snow that blankets
the landscape; the indents of trees, the hulking
of bushes. At dusk as sky darkens, starlings
come in their thousands, seasoned acrobats,
swirling and tumbling, shapeshifting in the sky.
Fish of air, shattering like glass, shards flying everywhere.
Awash with visible light, the spectrum of the sun
is streaked with Fraunhofer's dark lines,
blue becomes scattered, magenta cannot be seen.

* Mudra Position is a symbolic gesture in Japanese Buddhism
  & Hinduism.
* Fraunhofer Lines are a set of spectral lines in physics which
  correspond to chemical elements in the solar spectrum.

Letter from the Attic

Today I write to you, I can say
the unspeakable, can utter words
that echo and lie on white paper
like starfish on a beach.
Yesterday storms blew in from the east,
the beach at Lissadell was covered
with hundreds of floundered sea stars,
as if sky had plummeted to earth.

Some siren song sounded on the strand
and lured them here, I never heard it,
but heard the sigh of wind as it fingered
the marram grass, the swish of sea on sand.
Lissadell, how that name reverberates,
history strikes off Benbulben like a bell.
The mountains' giant shadow thrown
on the fields, the strand, the bay,
is like a binding thread of voice,
the ravel of language, the weave
of a story that overshadows.

These starfish are grounded here
on the sand past Goose Field where countless
geese landed from the faraway Arctic.
Sea and sky blended like an old grief healing,
gathering together the ragged edges
of loss to make it whole again.
All this I write to you from the quiet of my attic,
wherever you are, look up and see those stars.

Dear Reader Seamus Heaney
Doesn't Own Them

He doesn't own the talking stones, the bog, the forge.
I write poetry of my own, I too had a doorway in the dark,
the ringing metal, the falling meteoric light.

Mention a blackbird or St. Kevin and people say:
Oh that's in a Heaney poem and I reply:
He doesn't own the words. I too have gone

blackberry picking, gorged myself on purple clots
torn my skin to a red tattoo on briars hooks
and felt the urge to write about it.

But know that if I do, all that will be heard is Heaney.
I have lived my life near the Dodder river,
and like to write about it,

thankfully he has never mentioned it,
but I shuddered when his mate Muldoon did.
I spent my childhood trawling the gravel

of its shallow river bed, searching for slimy
frogspawn, with thick string lassoed
around my wrist and the jam-jars neck.

I examined my mother's borrowed basin,
and just like Heaney in Mossbawn
watched for the jellied mess to tadpole darken.

He had his childhood and I had mine,
he had Derry, I had Dublin. I too can write about the wind,
the mass and mothers' without cribbing him.

It all started with his Death of a Naturalist in '66,
I know that he is master of the trocee,
the alexandrine, the long breath.

Writers like to mine the golden seam of childhood;
freight our words to carry the heart's message,
and if that involves schoolbags, and forges

(mine was on the Terenure Road), and even
the brief coruscating light of frogspawn
so much the better. With all these words flying
try to remember Seamus Heaney doesn't own them.

Sometimes

Sometimes the air dissolves
around a thing and it stands clear,
of air, of shadows, we see it bare.
Sometimes time comes unstrung,
like a rope of milky opals spilling
unexpected flashes of kingfisher colours,
the jade green, the crimson throat,
before it slots back in.

Sometimes the sea stands still
for a brief moment, when the forward
push and pull of the undertow hushes
and the sand sparkles with airy foam
and pebbles idle. And in those times
we stand alone clear of the pressing chatter,
the urgency of now, and sometimes wonder
why the stars are where they are.

Leitmotif

Late summer thickens in a room
filled with empty chairs
where through the green of wild garlic
and the tall stems of purple teasel
a peacock goes. He seems to fan himself,
his gorgeous Argus-eyed tail aglow.
His iridescent Indigo blue almost
blinding us.

Grandmother sits like Iris
amongst the bodiless chairs,
using the spiny head of a teasel pod
to comb a rainbow coloured cardigan,
fulling the nap, making it glabrous.
Her patterns as intricate as the ceiling's
stucco work. While outside Greengages
slowly ripen, come September they will sweeten
in the long shadows of summer gone.

Summer Preserved

As you unscrew the lid,
a small puff of air,
the smell of summer
potted in a jar
of damson jam warms
the winter breakfast table.
We taste the orchard
on our tongues and sit
with plates of stickiness
spread on toast that looks
like purple crazy glazing.
The sullen air lightens,
our hands remember
the itch of nettle rash,
our irritation at
the news from the radio
dissipates.
We imagine damsons
slowly swelling in the sun
as winter ripens like a plum.

Hunting Truffles

Throw out the maps, the charts, the plans
go like truffle hunters out from dusk to dawn,
sniffing and searching under trees
in damp woods; the willows, oaks, elms.
Dig for White Gold imbued with the taste
and tang of earth, of pepper, of fungus,
breath in the musky smell.

From this you will know there are no
absolutes winnow your memories,
unstitch your loves, ruffle your senses,
dream of the Spanish Virgin,
Virgen de los Delores, resplendent in velvet,
her crown glowing gold and then throw
them all like windlestraws out onto air
and see what floats and see what falls.

Fragments

(A whirring of wings down the sky)

We will start with Sappho:
Love shook my heart
like the wind on the mountain
troubling the oak trees.

My oak tree is troubled, my husband
out gallivanting on the ride-on-mower
broke three years of green growth,
a clean snap, the sap stopped rising.
I tend its wound, retie the black halter.

There is an venerable oak on Elba,
or *Isola de Elba* as Napoleon knew it
when he sought shade from the boiling
sun under its nurturing arms.
When sailing the Tyrrhenian sea
having lately left the coast of Amalfi
I thought I spied its uppermost branches.

Be just, my lovely swain, and do not take
Freedoms you'll not to me allow, said Aphra Bhenn,
not playing any games, agent 160
as she was also named. She revealed
the DeWitts' plan to burn wooden ships
docked in the Thames.

This was transmigration indeed, never
mind the souls who sail the seven seas.
In a mangrove swamp of eerie trees,
roots exposed and everywhere grey mud
oozed, the world decomposed while we watched
our step on slippery boards.

In another light Aurora Borealis flashed
its pea green glow about the sky. Adam and
Eve stand in a hum of desire under an oak tree
whispering about how it was all going to be DNA
from that day forth.

my mother never had a television, fridge, or phone,
didn't ever dream of mobiles, computers,
iPods. Now our houses are full of bytes and modems,
at night the LED lights glow. When anything breaks
it is replaced, we go shopping,

to sail on silver moving stairs that buckle and repeat
up to the novel and new. In a Chinese whisper of need
we view motionless mannequins whose mouths
are stopped in a wordless O, then push through
other shoppers like swimmers in a crowded
pool, afraid we are on collision course and that we
might glance the arm or leg of a fellow swimmer.

Inside the dream the glittering coffee machines
are lined up like the Red Army advancing.
While we finger Venetian crystal,
the espressos hiss alarm and steam
as if the trembling glass held hemlock
and not just air, albeit expensive air;
we look blank as mannequins.
Again I think of my mother and the enduring oak
of my family tree, how quickly we leave all but our DNA.

Out again into the market place and busy streets,
at the end of Henry Street stands the Spire;
our soaring homage to the god of commerce and of sky;
its pinnacle thin as the wood of a spindle tree.
Outlined against bright sky, a giant steel needle
daily stitches the heavens and this earth together.

Tomorrow is the first day of Lent,
who will be first to renounce the virtual chorus
and silence the tweets and calls,
lose the constant contact we have through the waves
and like the swimmers or indeed Adam and Eve
reject the void and brush against the flesh
of one another?

Tell me what now, above all,
Your frantic heart desires.

Whatever the Weather

The day after the storm we noticed water
reaching right up to the flood
mark. With the receding morning tide
it had drawn back the line against
bladderwrack thrown up by stormy weather;
weed and debris on the beach sparkled in light.

When morning filled the room with light
we woke from dreams of water
tuned in the radio to hear the weather.
An announcer talked about the flood
while we entangled our sleepy limbs against
the bed end, holding back the tide.

We are late. A quick tumble will have to tide
us over; you rain kisses light
on me and hold me close against
your chest. Outside the sea is at low-water
hundreds of hungry gulls flood
the sand, for the booty of stormy weather.

Marriages made on earth have to weather
the daily flotsam of a running tide,
sometimes old arguments threaten to flood
back and we try to keep conversations light.
Currents of riptides do not hold water
when we have things to kick against.

Put in this backdrop, landscape against
the joys and trials of marriage can be heavy weather.
Years can pass like so much water
flowing under a bridge; small comforts tide
us over. Passion ebbs but light
can be brought to bear when memories flood.

Outside remains of yesterday's flood
throw rainy squalls hard against
the window, sometimes obscuring light.
It is like marriage, this constantly changing weather.
Our children are almost grown, then a turning tide
will favour us to float our boat in calmer water.

Now let our lives flood with undiminished light
and do not worry whether or not, we row against
the tide, we are happy to have dipped our toes in the water.

Decorating

A ladder's silver legs ascending
and descending, me straddling
the summit. Specks of paint flake our eyes
as together we go at stripping the walls
slicking a sweat to remind me
of the old delight that springs back
and glosses into life. Brushes
converging in an urgency
of now perform a choreographed
dance,   slow,   slow,
quick, quick,
                    slow
pulsing light across the waiting walls.
Air thrums taut as a newly skinned drum;
dusty scraps of waxy moths beat time
on the double glazing clouding it –
a small weather front patterning
the window glass. Your hands brushing
my skin colouring it in dappled light,
Water Lily White flaring
like the aluminium ladder rungs; paint spilt
left pooling on the floor.

Skinny Dipping

I'm Irish, we keep our clothes on
most of the time. We perform
contorted dances on beaches in Cork,
or Donegal; undressing under
not-yet-wet-towels. Worried that any gap
might expose us, lay some body-part bare.
It was the Immaculate Conception that did it,
if Mary could conceive a child without
removing her knickers, then by God
the rest of us could undress and swim
without baring our buttocks.
We swam serene in freezing seas,
goose bumps freckling our pale skin.
We lay togged out on wet sand desperate
for the weak sun to dry us, before performing
the contorted dance in reverse. Now as I
remove my clothes, peel them off
layer by layer down to the bare,
a brief moment of unease before the release
of water baptising skin. With a quiet 'Jesus, Mary',
I dive in.

Lazy Dogs, Quick Foxes

This is for the girls who were relegated
to the back of the class where they pinged
paper bombs from elastic bands
and balanced precariously on two legs
of their tilted chairs.

Who sat trapped in an agony of impatience
hormones hopping, budding breasts
restrained, strapped into the tight
bodice of a uniform.

For the others who paid attention
there would be the reward of banking,
teacher training or even the *law*.
For us there was always *secretarial*.

There we learned touch typing,
our fingers seeking blindly to master
the QWERTY layout
of a colour-coded keyboard.

Each key covered with little stickers
in rainbow shades. Like a guessing game
or three card trick, we had to pick the correct letter.
Slowly, we learned to type.

With time we gathered up a rhythm.
The satisfying sound of each key's light smack
as it was tapped, the ring to indicate end of line,
the singing of the carriage return

all set up a music of their own.
The apex we aimed for was seventy *doubleyoupeem*.
For months we crawled along adagio
happy just to hit the hidden letters revealed

like hieroglyphs on a snowy landscape
in triplicate. Our clean white sheets smeared
navy by carbon paper and slicked
ink black from the ribbon.

We slogged away until graduation day.
A minimum of thirty five *doubleyoupeem*.
before we could escape into our marked
lives and of course a perfect:
Quick Brown Fox Jumps Over The Lazy Dog.

Rosebud

The only doll I ever wanted was black,
dressed in white lace for communion
or maybe a wedding. Not like the black babies
we gave our precious pennies to,
eschewing treats we could have eaten.
Sweets, the nuns said would taste of sugared guilt.

We thought the black-habited nuns bald
beneath their white wimples, only for
that halo of brightness they could have
been witches. I called my doll Rosebud,
her black hair was waved like perms
women wore then in the Fifties.

Unless blessed with curls we schoolgirls
wore ours straight with skewed fringes
cut by our mothers' impatient hands.
Eventually the urge to experiment grew too much,
I popped Rosebud's doll eye out in an botched
operation, I sheared her lashes, none grew back.

She was still beautiful, but inert, lovely dark cheeks
and red tipped lips. Later I lopped the fingers
from her right hand. She didn't even murmur
when I mentioned appendix. That operation
proved too complex, her torso being made
of sterner stuff than her more pliable limbs.

Eventually I let her be, left the nuns
and moved on from black babies and butchering;
to sins of lust for boys gifted with the glad eye
and cursed with heads of greasy hair. I thought maybe
I could work on them instead. I always asked
about their appendix, my fingers itching to fix them.

Postcard Perfect

In an old John Hinde postcard of Rosslare
Harbour stand three figures, one in a swimsuit
two others by the sea. One of them could
be me. The mailboat in the background
docked at the harbour mouth waits for
the Dublin train. It was June, two girls of thirteen,
our mothers' sent us to the Strand alone,
our first time away from home.

The landlady in our B&B had two sons,
exotic, different than the jeering Dublin boys.
We explored the hills and cliffside,
climbed rocks, dipped our toes in trepidation
into a freezing sea. We rowed a small boat
each pulling the oars, wood against wood,
wood against water, sunburnt I learnt to swim
as playfully we dared each other to jump in.

At night the lighthouse out at Tuskar Rock
lit the bedroom as I tossed restless, skin on fire;
limbs heavy and tired from rowing, caught
in its warning glare I avert my eyes alive
with longings I could not name no matter how I tried.

Stings

The sight in the mirror of midge bites
shaped like Orions' belt
circling my waist,
glowing and star shaped,
stung my memory, made me
think of a long ago orchard.

Late September, the fruit
had swelled all summer, puffed up
and hung with sugar sweetness
in the heat. I had snuck into this Eden
not yet able to reach
the higher branches where red apples
or yellow pears still clung on,
the rest plucked for the table
or windfalls squashed under-foot.

A sudden snap of sticks,
crunch of leaves, mush of bruised fruit
a sinister sound, an angry buzz
at my ankles: I had stumbled
on a wasps nest.
Some ancient instinct kicked in,
surprising myself I leapt for the wall
and like a hero from some TV show,
cleared it in one go.

As I vaulted the stone wall
my shirt pulled from my jeans
exposing virgin skin.
when I reached home,
fruitless and bedraggled,
I felt and saw an angry girdle
of wasp stings, below my budding
breasts, star watermarks
circling my waist.

Letter from the Attic II

Again I write to you
about the elaborate smash and grab
burnt orange of the Kingfisher,
the jolt of electric blue.

High in my dusty room moats dance
gilded in midas glitter that gleams through
the Velux roof light. Rough beams
above my head hold up grey slate tiles

and my pen darts
like the fisher king across an expanse
of remembered water.
I try to unpack my words for you,

strip them to the tangible simplicity
of the shy bird, the sight of whom
on any day snags our eye
and holds it.

POETRY LIBRARY

It Will All End In Tears

(for Marian)

Cross words, raised voices, phone clamped
to her ear, unseen stoop, high step,
long drop. Hospital stop, admission, operation.

The algebra of broken bones
resolved by metal plate and steel pins.
Home with her leg in a sarcophagus of plaster.

Aluminium crutches, rubber stopped,
she hops painfully. Three children under eight,
domestic disaster. Defeated by the high
tide of the threshold,

her white cast hovering in surrender like flags
of bog cotton, her *to have and to hold* husband,
swearing an oath, carries her,
his old/new bride, over it again and again.

All Leaving by the Same Door

Everything I do now must be done
in a hurry there is so little time
remaining then I will be gone
I have just realised we are all dying
Rumours of rain come to me
through the ether a flood of memory
pushing past the breakwater
to sink me Why are the iridescent
innards of a shell called *mother-of-pearl*
all that grit and bother is that what
makes the Abalone its mother
I need my mother now
Now do you hear
My thought are in a flurry
a rush of love unstinting
I must hear the held note
the octave's steps and half-steps
stretching out to nothingness
Quick sound out the dots and dashes
of an SOS a palindrome
I guess as it runs back on itself
in dizzying circles
I am going down can you hear
Down into the failing light
I must take hold of my life.

Hell Reinstated, Devil–may–care
(Ex Cathedra)

Its back, he said. I wondered where it went.
Where had it been all this time, perhaps tapping
out a beat, an idea, an absence of grace.

Hell is real, its official, its not just other people.
It is a proper place, the flames bright as ever,
the Pope says so and he should know he's infallible.

Hell burns forever, hellfire never goes out.
It is a burning lariat about our hearts
to keep us in check, hold us in thrall.

Lambent the everlasting fire licks at us.
Damns us all to hell and back
The Pope he knows he's got the inside track.

A Small Slip

Searching for a misplaced iPad
in corners not looked in for years,
like a tear in time my fingers found
a small slip of browning cardboard
and there, not seen in ages my Father's
firm writing. A list of radio stations,
their bands and wavelengths noted
and numbered from the days
when the tuning knob travelled
the glass panel. I can see his hand
adjusting and re-adjusting, shuffling
this way and that seeking arias
in the static. I now trace the numbers,
place my prints over his as if I could locate
his music through the atmospheric
interference of time flown, his handwriting
speaking volumes in a sudden hum
of clarity from a far-flung place.

The Bodies Exhibition

We queued a little guiltily to see the Exhibition
reminiscent of a Victorian freakshow.
Real dead bodies like we have never seen
them before. Preserved in silicone
exposing tissue, tendons, veins,
a flap of skin held back
like the opening of a show tent inviting us
to take a closer look at the bearded
lady, the double headed man.

It seems simple to us with our
advanced technologies, our stealing
of Promethian fire. We have found a way
to flense and flay people and reveal
Polymerised innards, they even show
the mystery of the womb, the birth canal.
Some exhibits are held in desiccated suspended slices,
like a stack waiting to be made whole again
without the specks in a Pitri dish.

Despite ourselves we are excited,
to be able to place our fingers
into the gaping wound and see
to the true heart of things.
Look there Thomas, no doubt,
we can almost get a handle on it.
Hearts are old news, we have a magnified
view of the Pineal gland, they even took the eyes
clean out of their dead heads for us to poke at.
They showed us almost everything,
though we looked and looked we saw neither
flutter nor wingbeat of a soul.

Thresholds, Doors and Floors

I could tell all the doors
by their different handles,
some smooth, one jangling,
another stiff and so on.

On entering a room with no light,
no colour to show me the way,
I could tell where I stood
by the lie of the floorboards,

some standing slightly proud,
one over by the window dipping a little,
near an edge of a rug close by the firegrate.
I knew my home better than the back

of my own hand, which changes
with age anyway and some days the hand
is shackled with rings, others it is bare
as the day it was born.

I recognised the dark green door of the room
I shared with my sister and its dusty damask rose
wallpaper flocking the walls. I knew how
the window caught on the lintel.

All is liminal, perception is marginal –
limbo, limbus, everything just hanging there.

Upper Cushina

(after a poem by Liza Jarrot)

You the cows and sheep of the fields
of Upper Cushina, you Upper Cushina
a lane not a street flanked by fields
filled with cows and sheep, you Spring
fill the deep, deep longing of the trees
in Upper Cushina to bud and blossom
just like the lambs of the sheep of Upper
Cushina and you my love who watches
the lambs of the sheep feed and bleat
and race around the bright fields, head butting
one another in brief Spring joy,
while the trees weep in the rain,
their feet rooted in the clabber of the bog
in Upper Cushina, and you and I walk
Lucky the dog on the bog in Cushina
while bullocks bellow for their Ma
in the fields with the trees in the Spring
and you and I sometimes long for city
streets, with pavements and street lights
and bright nights not found in the bog
and fields of Upper Cushina.

Small Cow, Far Away Cow Perspective

(for Ardal O'Hanlon)

The far away cow seen in the distance
from my window is as small
as the green plastic farmyard
animals, I played with as a child.

A tangled nest of yellow thread
was toy hay, a bottle lid the drinking
trough, a little cardboard box the stable
and all the minute animals placed

strategically around the side table
in the livingroom. If I squint in parallax
I can contort the real far away cow
to hop magically from one field

to another clearing the fence in an instant.
I turn back to my kitchen and brew tea,
pour the water, fuss the teabag brown
and when I turn again

far away cow had become near cow
and transformed into a giant on me.

On The Line

Our train from Edinburgh delayed
by a death on the line, I recalled
that girl who knelt on a track
hands joined as if in prayer, and I'd read how
the driver never drove another train,
said he would see her forever
at the moment of impact as he screamed
to an unheeding God and the wheels skidded
on the iron tracks. At last we were underway,
this lost time a slight annoyance in our day
soon gave over to the healing sight of
fast moving coastline.

Small inlets flanked by headlands
gave glimpses down to the sea,
waves juddering on the pebble beach.
A hawk holds itself still in the thermals
its wingspan two hands splayed
visually tracking its prey, almost in line
with our window, as he hovers over sea-spray;
then, as if we were derailed
an unexpected tunnel cuts the light in two,
just as suddenly we emerged and journeyed on.

Pulling out of Newcastle I glanced up
from my book and saw wooden wings
thrown wide, *Angel Of The North*,
Gormleys' angel holding its own on a hillside
in stinging rain and buffeting winds
casting its shadow deep.
We sped on in a blur of fields, sea and sky
and wondered where exactly
on this track did someone choose today
to die, while we wait for the end of the line.

My Mother Ate Electricity

Sometimes, on stormy nights, I think of you
how death persuaded you in increments
and not as a bolt out of the blue.
Your mind a landscape blazing with bushfires
until they nailed you in place, fed volts
into your brain and bound it up in haywire.
Said they cleared the mists, didn't tell
of the smoke shrouding your eyes.

Opiates lay like wafers on your tongue,
all the black hate gone, as were the songs
and memories; babies caged in cots
waited for your care, our endless cries
seared your brain until the doctor applied
the shocks again and again, whitened your bones
and cauterized the sound. The babies called
as if from an oubliette and you left
eating handfuls of forgetting.

The Backward Step

We need to wind things back,
put time in reverse, loop the ravelled
ribbon, fill the spool with thread again.
We need to empty out your grave,
backfill the hole that gaped,
spit out the Obol and let the wind restring
your voice with new, clear breath.
I will leave the blizzard of your still body
coffined on the table in the living room,
undo the shroud pins and remove
the brown Franciscan robe.
Who's idea was that anyway?

Let us start that day over.
No fight from me this time when you drive
up on your motor scooter, your short hair
helmeted around you to where I wait;
a bad tempered teenager at a bus stop.
I will draw my unicorn horn back in,
turn my cheek the other way
and receive your healing kiss. We will sit
in the June sun together in our summer frocks
and restring the beads of all the lives
that warped to accommodate your loss.
You will live to a fine old age,
and I, your daughter, will in turn mother you.

Lost Voice

'Once the ivory box is broken,
beats the golden bird no more'

EDNA ST. VINCENT MILLAY

That her body folds back on itself I can take,
the collapse of her lungs and final hiss of air.
I can imagine the last blink of her eyes
before they seal shut, one last look
at their blue/grey pupils already fixed, light
no longer able to enter. They say that nails
and hair still grow awhile, how do they know?

The brain stills as connections are unmade,
all thoughts, memories, everything goes.
That her ears can no longer hear I accept,
the snail shape closes itself to sound. The heart
slows then finally stops, bloods long haul through
the labyrinth of veins now over, not one
more drop goes round.

I know that the tongue is clogged by death,
gone are all the shrieks of rage, murmurs of love
and endearment, the songs and poetry,
blocked now by still lips that will never again
move to kiss. But the voice box what of it?
What if there was some way that breath could play
over it and sound out the tone, and tune,
and timbre of her voice?

Everything else I can remember,
but I cannot hear her speak, cannot
put words back into her quiet mouth,
she breathed life into me, now
life has squeezed her by the throat.

Paper Dolls

Strung out like a line of paper dolls,
your children tore and broke one by one,
you hung them up in tatters
of white paper ripped and ragged.

They swung like clothes sagging
from a washing line, wind blowing
through them as if it mattered,
but they held on.

Arms outstretched clinging to the lifeline
of the orange rope, strung from here
to there and only air in between.

At evening you unpeg all the papery scraps,
carry them carefully indoors
as if you were carrying torn children.

Last Things

Seeing him in the ward bed without
his broad framed out-of-date glasses,
makes him more naked than when undressed.

Their absence giving his face a slack look,
as if flesh were unhinging itself.
The lack of thick lenses blurring his eyes

makes them look like rainclouds collecting off
to the east. Death gathers itself around him.
His shrinking body parchment against crisp sheets.

Faded flowers stink in vases, television racketing reality TV,
visitors gather raucous around some other bed
life expands and busies itself.

While pulled curtains are the only things
that stand between my father and his skew-ed
view of an ignominious end.

Memento Mori

I am surrounded by the belongings
of ghosts. The custodian of memory:
I have my dead sister-in-law's writing slope,
my friend's mother's blue cornflowers
were moved from their clay in Wicklow
and interred in my garden.
Then there are all the goods and chattels
that my parents owned; my father's retirement
gold pen, resplendent in its slim velvet
lined box, my mother's marriage band
has circled my finger for more years than
I care to remember. I have her Arklow china plates,
their orange poppies waving like a troop
of flag-raising soldiers.

I have become the keeper of the flame,
the keepsake holder. I have granny's green
tea pot on my shelf, no tea leaf revelations
spouting from its narrow mouth, carrying news
from wherever she has gone, along with her scent
of 4711. My house and heart and head
are teeming with the thoughts and belongings
of the dead, who float around me cluttering
the shelves and are dug in deep
flourishing in my flower beds.

Hatching The Vision

On the embossed wallpaper
in my daughter's room
pages torn from a school atlas
are pinned to the furred design.
Arrows curve across countries and seas,
a life lived forward. A frieze
of laurel leaves decorates the border,
she is trying to gain some traction
on the wide world, find her footing.
No atlas moth will eat holes in her,
no moss will gather, she is on the move,
a stone rolling. Her cocoon walls
are expanding, next the roof might take off
and sail to far-flung places.
The looped lines cleave the atlas
like swallows slicing evening air;
or a sword loose from its scabbard
carving the world into manageable pieces
out beyond its frame of shining leaves
and stitching them into the wide clear blue.
With wind in her pockets the trajectory
of those pointing arrows are aiming
at a future for now just visualised.
They say clearly as any cartography:
I'm outta here.

POETRY LIBRARY

Clear Water

No memories waiting to ambush
and snare her back, her short lived
life still gathered cogent around her.
None of it as yet too far behind –
how free she is. Does she know
how to grasp it, land it like a salmon
grassed? Life will loosen her grip,
time, that fickle fish will trickle
through her finger tips
like the gasping salmon
sloughing off her sequinned skins
until the papery husk's revealed.
All the netted hours and moments blown
to dusty scraps. Her lived life
drowned – ashes in her gaping mouth.
Swim, we call to her breathlessly,
urgently, *swim on for your dear life*.

Brown Trout

Mayfly were performing their last dance
as evening streaked blood-red across the river,
midges were worrying our ears and scalp,
you cradled an oar loosely in the oarlock.

Then we saw him, he must have sheltered
near the overhang of the clay bank, waiting for day
to cool; a huge brown trout, coloured Rubens Madder,
his shape tricked out in fading light.

He snapped at the lure, the line ran tight,
you struggled to hold him as he fought,
the thin nylon pulled taut, his heavy jaw jutting,
his reddish, orange skin glowing, his whole being

concentrated into a spinning leap. The cruel hook held,
you reeled him close and lifted him from the cool
water, brought the blade across the jumping
line and cut him free, bloodied but still swimming.

Lovely Trees

Outlined in level light
blunt cut ends of trees
are stacked in a high wooden
wall of culled timbers, shorn of
leaf and limbs. All we can see is
rounded histories, in bud-like tight
whorls the middle broadening
out in concentric ripples
like so many secrets
growing larger as
they age.

Lost Things

Things go missing
around here,
the funneling wind carries them off
while we tend
to other things.
Today my green plastic watering-can
has vanished.
I've looked behind the shed
and under the forsythia
and no sight of it.
Now I note the bird-feeder
has gone too,
flown off somewhere
I cannot see.
The watering-can
and bird-feeder are together
having a talk about loss.
These are the small,
incremental losses that collect behind us
and gather through our lifetime
into a black death hole
where all the lost things
are stored and wait to snare us,
some day when our
thoughts are elsewhere,
and wind us.

The Golden Mean
(or 1.61803399)

About my neck a dead aunt's gold chain
so wide it's almost a collar.
There is a framed picture of her wearing it,
burnished under the relentless African sun.

She lived her adult life on the shifting
continent of Africa, that name changing place
looked for in the atlas on rainy afternoons
in Dublin. I search today for those missing
names; Zaire, Abyssinia
even Rhodesia all changed now.

In the photo she has gypsy-dark hair,
surprising, as except for one other brother
the rest of us are fair. Almost leached out,
as if we, and not she were bleached in foreign
light. Dressed in uniform, bull-whip in hand
she bloody play-acts at Empire, Queen and Crown
clinging on in dusty outposts as we scan
fly-blown maps.

And felt smug back then that our young and green
Republic did not need imprimatur from
a neighbouring young Queen. Thinking our names
were permanent and not just versions
in the transmigration from Gaelic to English
and sometimes back again seeking shelter
in the caves of our mouths.

She never did come home, I wear her
golden tether into a new millennium,
a different world, where I found the Congo,
Ethiopia and Zimbabwe, everything changed
and everything stayed the same.

Baggage

Under the bed a brown leather suitcase
of secrets and memories masquerading
as clothes crammed in. Full to the brim.

We lift the lid to unpack; grief leaps
to ambush. We never know how deep we're in
'til we try to dig ourselves out.

We start at the top with the frocks and work
our way back through the pile,
pinafore dresses rucked at the front, criss-
crossed tight stitches a fist in a child's heart.

This case and its contents smell of mildew,
tainted with rot and dis-ease, moving
through layers to the teen years.

The short shifts, bell bottoms, mirrored skirts.
Her dead in a box, a Pandora's treasure
trove trunk. Then come the lost years

fake furs, fake everything, a discarded Biba dress
reminds us of the seventies, where, on achingly
beautiful beaches in Greece, we sunned ourselves
naked, not a stitch, no remains.

Grief an ill fitting garment shrouding our pain,
discarded clothes once casually flung now stun,
dishevelled dresses throng, losses worn lightly,

blush silk under-garments a thin second skin.
Unfashionable threads spring the trap of memory.
This suitcase is giving up ghosts.

A Last Note

Although we lived at least
five miles inland, when fog
came we heard the warning horn
low and mournful. We shivered
in our beds and drew the blankets
around us snug in its boom.

While at sea sightless ships were signalled
by notes tuned through the reeds
to let a captain reckon his course,
warn him not to blunder shore-wards.

Like the noise of trains tunnelling
through the night, the fog horn held
us in thrall. On New Years' Eve
even if the air was clear, bells
rang out and mingled with horns,
all hell let loose to welcome in the year.

Blue Bobbin

Its dull case an ornament
in the corner, its use almost
forgotten. someone has taken
the table of the Singer Sewing
machine, once everyone had one.
If you lifted it out you could turn
the handle instead of footing
the treadle. Gone, along
with the table is the drawer
that held bobbins, my delight,
as a child sifting the
spools of rainbow thread.

When my mother sewed
she favoured the blue bobbin.
All our curtains, whatever the colour,
were backed with blue stitches.
I helped her thread the needle
through a maze of eyes and hooks
down to where the thread vanished
into a small silver box.
Like a magician pulling an endless
stream of hankies from his sleeve;
it conjured another thread
and together, they and we,
formed the stitch.

At night when mother was busy
I used to slide the lid on the silver
chamber to see if I could figure out its trick.
I only saw the small half-moon lever
moving back and over
and like a hidden slice of sky,
the edge of a blue bobbin peeping out.

Hidden Things

The stories are there to be read in the skeletons,
bones will tell tales. You have to work hard
to imagine their bleached whiteness
whispering from the dark soil, the waterlogged bog.

In the short days of winter they cry out
jangling and noisy, ghost-like in their clamour
disembodied in the rolling mist.

The earth we stand on is spongy under our weight
held up only by aeons of bones knitted together
like a huge trampoline that gives and gives back
as the centuries pile up under our feet.

Think of Flodden's fields, the bloody banks
of the Boyne, Somalia's red earth, the mud of the Somme,
the shifting sands at Louisburgh.

Occasionally bones reveal themselves,
rattling tibias and fibulas, carpals and metacarpals,
the clavicles and ribs fleshed out they nudge our conscience
with their numinous presence

their shocking clarity and then nervously
we dance on them, dance on the curve of the earth
caught out of the corner of our eyes.

Cicatrix

The farmer passes on the lane, she slows
her jeep and greets us, her waxed mac
is strewn with feathers, her knitted black cap
pulled far down could be a balaclava
and for a moment we are back
before the peace, back to the dangers
of unapproved lanes and narrow roads
that criss-crossed the border.

She is like a mixed message, idling with
her engine running, and stuck as she is
with feathers, (it is turkey plucking season)
and that hat almost masking her,
but the army green of her old jeep would not fit.
A pheasant breaks cover from a culvert,
and runs amok his quick-fire burst of 'kirk, kirk,'
startles us. We laugh to camouflage our fright.

Keeping Shtum

Easter silence must have been such a relief
for mother. For three hours on Good Friday
not a squeak, not a peep out of us.

Six children who usually hollered
and yelled engaged now in fierce,
unspoken competition.

The sacred hours between twelve and three,
when Christ hung in his death throes
between the guilty as hell thieves.

We ran the scenes in our heads,
the heavy cross, the long climb in the heat,
dust and sweat mingling with blood

as the thorny crown bit deep: and then
the nails piercing flesh, the agony as
he hung broken and dying. Dead.

Our childish delight in recounting this
to ourselves, not a word escaping
our parched and sealed lips.

We had already done the hard time of Lent,
giving up sweets for forty days
almost crucified us.

We were not going to fall at this last station.
Our older brother; in an imitation of the soldier
dipping the vinegared sponge into Christ's wounds,

tickled us mercilessly, in a bid to make us break.
But we had our eyes fixed on the main prize,
a surfeit of confectionary eggs on Easter Sunday

and the satisfaction of knowing our hard won
silence had helped that gaunt man to rise
and roll back the rock. Healed and victorious

while we reassumed our noisy din,
quietened now and then by mouths
overflowing with melting chocolate.

Trouble

See the poppets made of hair
fashioned by her hand
to work like a wand.

They muttered witch
say she's a bitch
but not in her hearing.

She keeps rabbit's feet
for a charm, says
where's the harm?

None if you're not the rabbit.
Still no one will cross her,
ask what's her game?

Know that their name
will end stuck on a pin,
they'll get lumps –

shingles will pickle their skin.
The whole town is alarmed
held in the thrall

of her jingles and snares,
rumours of Frozen Charlottes
ruckling her walls.

The water is tainted
it tastes of garlic,
slightly metallic.

We think of the hair poppets,
the ghostly Charlottes
then smile to her face and hurry on,
wish she'd be gone.

Euphemisms

Back then everyone was evasive,
saying nothing was the name of the game.
Illnesses were revealed in gestures
and euphemisms, like a game of Charades.

My mother was poorly, it was her *Nerves*,
they were shredded, she was *Losing
her Marbles*. Would not heal. They came at her
with all their bells and whistles.

Held her head in a vice, threw
their jolts and sizzles, fogged
her already befuddled brain
with floods of electricity.

She hated it. The scorched earth
of her mind trying to right itself
suggested a rainbow of pills
one swallow and she was gone.

They tried the cure on me
five times, but on my heart not my head,
clamped my arms and legs
in jelly moulds, to protect my bones.

Then when my back was turned,
my eyes closed, they flicked a switch,
did the burn. Annealed with blue electric,
like her I resisted, this quivering heart's my own.

Ablation

They want to thread
my Femoral artery
shuttle a line all the way
to my heart
like some bizarre
sewing lesson.

They say it's to break
the crook circuit,
scratch its surface.
Silk purse, Sows ear?

Throttle

They wore lead aprons, held
a small Pandora's chest aloft
like a miniature coffin. They opened it
slowly, nothing flew out.

Nestled in sponge a needle
the size of Cleopatra's and
spiky as a splinter. A little prick
and it's over they soothed.

Cradled in my clavicle
the butterfly of my thyroid
had turned, needed to be burned.
They nuked my neck

it felt naked, stricken.
When they left
I heard white noise
a flutter of recoiling wings.

Rowing

Swaying over the boathouse
budded oak trees echoing
long bow-shaped planks
of the craft below.
We push out with an oar
from dark of boathouse
to light of lake.
At depth the water darkening,
away to the left startled swans
take flight in a drawn out curve
of white wing breaking loose
against sky. We dip and pull
heavy blades sculling through
currents. We follow
the circumference of the lake,
pushing through tangles
of water-lilies, the white cups
of their voluptuous flowers
blaze like flags for a day.
Fish break the surface skin
with a leap
so sudden we miss it,
seeing only rings spooling out
in concentric ripples making
and unmaking the shadow picture
of the tall trees circling the water.
We catch the flash of delicate
blue damsel flies darting amongst reeds,
and hear the wash and slurp of water.
Framed by trees our shoulder blades
rhythmically heave. Dipping arms
catch knees as oars slice water
and midges madden skin and scalp,
light starts to fade and land beckons,
we row back.

All That Jazz

Why did you go there, I asked her,
what for? She looked at me as if
I were stupid. *You know* —
but I didn't, couldn't understand
the look of hurt in her grey eyes.
I remember seeing them like that
before, when she was a child
and going past our gate had noticed
an arm pointing to the sky,
protruding from under the lid
of the bin. She gave it a yank,
it was Raggedy Anne, she rescued her,
desperately trying to brush
the dirt of potato peel and tea leaves
from Raggedy's round moon face.
Her eyes had that same faraway
hurt look then as now.
Again I tried, *But Why?* She looked
at me with a shrug, For love, she said,
her face taking on like the moon,
For love and all that Jazz.

Dear Diary

After, when we had all stopped wanting to be
Anne Frank, when we had spent nights writing
our diaries and were bored with our life stories,
Amy Johnson was our big thrill. We could
picture her still, up there, flying high.
You had to die to be a heroine.

Then we all got interested in boys
put away our toys of childhood, pouted
our lips, widened our eyes. Our friends' spotty
older brother, whom last year we thought of
as clumsy and a bother, now became
an object of desire. We licked our lips
on lead pencils and wrote Dear Diary
as if our engines were on fire.

I Just Want To Add

(after William Carlos Williams)

But why were
those plumbs
in the icebox,
losing their ripe

sweetness?
They should be kept
warm, on a sunny
window sill.

Still, I did eat them,
they *were* sweet,
delicious and
so very, very cold.

Miss Carr's Junior School in Rathgar

We began by learning the alphabet
quickly we got to know our place
in the scheme of things. Mary Andrews
always held her hand up first.

it felt unfair that I didn't come second in the roll call,
my surname began with B, a little bitty
apostrophe in-between and the O more like
a soft breath than part of my name.

Kind Miss Carr kept control with a thrown
tennis ball pocking us to attention
silencing our clucks and whispers
it netted us with its bounce.

Occasionally I would be called to clean
the blackboard, to swing the wooden eraser wide
across all the letters, wiping them
first to a blur, then to a democracy of obliteration

until at last no matter how carefully
I placed the chalky duster down,
a small puff of dust, mushroom shaped
rose from the atoll of Miss Carr's desk.

Years later and long-left school on a trip
to Pompeii, seeing all those O shaped mouths
choked with pumice dust appalled me
and brought the classroom blasting back.

Where I had to sit fettered, palms flat on the desk,
while Miss Carr moved painfully past
what I thought of as my rightful B,
and dragged on for another unlucky thirteen letters

'til finally I got to raise my hand and call in the affirmative
as Gaeilge. Anseo for the O in O'Brien.

Attachment

*(In China red painted eggs, symbols of fertility and good luck
are given to friends and family for honouring a child's birth)*

A long awaited phone call from the adoption agency,
your daughter has arrived, check your email.
She came as an attachment, already born.

We tried to bring her image into focus, scan her face.
The picture was like a magicians trick, interlacing
she rises towards us through the ether.

She is ghosting her way here in flickering lines,
This is the first time we have seen her
as she appears fully formed on screen.

We glimpse her mouth developing, her sleepy eyes
almond shaped emerging from the screen's snow-field,
images heaped like a cradle, we hear her trills and tweets.

We have a good connection, soon we will fly
to bring her home. Meanwhile we save the file,
store her carefully in a folder marked red-painted eggs.

Hinamatsuri - The Japanese Doll Festival

Nusha, our daughter loves the ceremony of the dolls,
the loving couple, the prince and princess seated
in tiered splendour at the apex, lolling like melons
with their robes puffed out around them,
painted faces almost smiling, lacquered lips red as cinnabar,
their night-dark hair is real and shines as if lit by stars.
Nusha brushes her hair until it glows, taps her wooden getas,
wriggles her toes. This is her day for praise and future-wish
our job is to guide her, watch her grow and push
her off into the river of life, like the dolls of long ago.
Ever year we stow them away, once made of straw,
but now something more substantial, something lasting.

The next row seats five musicians, garb not as sumptuous,
as the royalty, but gorgeous nonetheless, each one holds
an instrument that Nusha says she can hear, hear the strings,
hear them sing. Our ears are too old for such sounds;
we listen as leaves rustle in trees, and a tumult of traffic goes by.
The last step holds the helpers, clothes more like our own *Yukatas*;
plain, serviceable. They proffer the food, mochi sweets, peach
blossoms, brushes for the royal couples hair, oils and unguents.
Nusha holds a western doll, tall with golden hair, slim waist,
generous chest, she says I need to grow up soon, it's urgent.

Nesting Democracies

Hammamet beach is covered
in tiny jellyfish, a wreath of stings,
strength in translucent numbers,
they made the beach unusable.
Canute like sweepers try to hold back
the tide of them. In the hotel,
boys sing and sell pomander posies
of Jasmine, tightly tied white star flowers.

Bouazizi the street vendor with his barrow
sets himself and his country aflame,
A pungent, beacon lighting the night
gathering strength in numbers.
In Alexandria and Cairo and Suez
people stand and wait united by Facebook,
they repeat Bouazizi's name and still they stand.
The militia holster their guns.

They are their brothers, fathers,
sons. At home women watch and wait
behind doors, for the chink that will let the blade
of light enter. Strait is the gate, they twitter
amongst themselves in the shade of apricot trees
hearts lifted they stroke their daughters velvet hair
always living with contradictions.

Frayed dignities, nested freedoms,
the stings of an army of jellyfish,
the persistent scent of gathered jasmine,
a leaping sun, scorched flesh, tanks,
guns and television cameras:

 POETRY LIBRARY

Enough
Yizzi
Bass
Kifaya
Enough
and they hold
their breath,   and wait
still   standing.

Sanctuary

A buzz of busy streets, a shriek of tyres
on tarmac, we go underground to the thunder
of subway trains, down past ragged men with palms
outstretched, pleading for nickels and dimes,
past legless vets on low trollies sketching
scenes of high summer meadows, alive
with whirling dragonflies, passerines flying
over long grasses, dive-bombing black ticks
and insects. We climb back into bright
Mulberry Street to the cathedral, dwarfed
by so many circling buildings stretching
skywards. The brick and glass of Renwick's
gothic glory stands crowded but unbowed,
pointing steeples split the blue. We enter
through its high portals, our footfall echoing
Spellman's words – how every advancing step
brings heaven nearer. Outside noises fade
and we are bathed in bright candlelight
gleaming like a lost silver dollar.

Someone hands me a green palm from a table
strewn with fan shaped leaves. I do the old math,
it is the Sunday before Easter, when Christ
entered Jerusalem, the road under his donkey's
hooves strewn with palm. A line from a poem
learned in school hums in my head.
Fools! For I too have had my hour;
one short fierce hour and sweet.
The tabernacle glimmers on the altar,
the faithful quickly bowing and blessing
themselves, summonsing up images
from the ancient map of the heart in this quiet place.
It is as if earth's plates have shifted slightly
and the teeming streets outside are gone —

rubbed out and written over like a palimpsest,
though the Vets' lost legs are still heavy,
a ghostly echo. A bells' tongue flares
and rings out a sweet summer meadow song
while I stand in this sanctuary gifted with greenery.

Therefore Do Not Worry About Tomorrow

(Matthew 6:34)

for Lynn

You could be sleeping, curled in a dream
with only water in motion rocking you
like a shell that the sea has rocked open,
gritty sand lies on your lips and heart.
The blue of morning wide as an ocean
is shelter and the white sky is the starched
sheet covering you. Wires woven like
seaweed ensnare you, evening slips
into night, the ward bell seams up the day.
Tell your aching heart to heal, let the needles
and drips and monitors become obsolete.
For now, just lie easy like driftwood
sufficient unto the day.

Don't Look Down

We are waiting to board, stuck on the gangway
poised on the lip of the quay and port side
of the ship. Those ahead are already at sea,
behind them we are suspended, feet
no longer on dry land and looking through the gap
at black enamel water below.

We shuffle forward, bags in hand, this no-mans'
land holds us in thrall, we can move neither
fore nor aft, one slip and it's all over. We clutch
railing ropes like drowning people who cannot swim,
longing for welcoming hands to haul us in.
Being on this boarding plank is akin to being

on a makeshift raft, will it stay afloat between
the two worlds? Already with its weight of souls
we see it bow, we think the unimaginable;
slipping down between the new world
of the ship and hard luck land. Lost in the seadrift
no-one would hear our cries: the fall too far.

The gulls sharp shrieks more urgent to their ears,
the boom of the deep as it slaps off each side:
Don't Look Down!
Someone urges nervously. Look ahead, eyes forward!
Somewhere over the horizon is a new land.

At hooter sound, the logjam breaks,
the crowd rushes forward. Is this how
Brendan and the monks felt in their flimsy
craft as they pushed off from the last of land
on their perilous ocean voyage? And we like them
for just a moment still had a foot in both camps.

Lamping

It's exciting, staves off the boredom
of nights in with the wife, has a spice of danger,
a whiff of sulphur. Gunning the truck

lurching over ditches and stones, lamps
rigged on the roof, fingers itching the switch
ready to light up the dark.

Eyes strain for a sight of fox or hare.
Look! Look! see over there!
Triggers already cocked, feeling the steel,

readying for the shot. Transfixed in thousands
of watts, he goes down in a hail of pellets.
His heart exploding like an over-ripe plum.

He drops to the grass, they leave him behind
this was for fun, not for the pot; they drive on.
Lamps dimmed, fur and cartridges scattered.

Fossil Fuel

Seen from the kitchen window
a distant line of black plastic swaddling
sods of turf; billowing in the wind
illuminated by the glint of sun, makes them look
like carriages of a distant train hurtling past.
But it is just bog going nowhere. Away
near the skyline a new hotel is lit up like a tableau,
its arc lamps lighting the sky for miles.
They burn all night in a bright advertisement
for this hotel and golf links out here
in the middle of nowhere.
Who are they telling, or is it just whistling
in the dark for consolation? Night here is so black
that stars blaze and if you turn your back
on the hotels' harsh light you could be anywhere,
just another speck amid constellations
that burned up years ago, like we here below
are firing the last of turf
that took thousands of years
to grow, we scavenge like fossickers
gleaning desperately for gold.
At night down in the dark field a red glow,
that could be a coloured firefly
if such a thing were so, or red eye of fox,
but no, it is the light of a battery powering up
the electric fence that keeps us all in our place.

Skating

Each day we wake it seems colder,
mornings now white-out in hoar-frost or snow.
We go walking to the lake to see if we can skate,

unheard of in these parts, but its been
freezing for so long. Gingerly we toe the ice,
looking for the tell-tale flow of ripples melting,

of water undulating as we apply light pressure
before chancing it and stepping full on,
hoping it will hold, we push out

into the middle and start our ice-dance,
minute by minute we grow bolder,
sliding this way and that

cutting intricate patterns with our blades.
We twist and spin, invert our feet, abruptly turn
and slice the surface see weed lying low beneath,

over near the other shore bulrush heads are waving,
leaking cotton like white flags
of warning or surrender. We are spinning tops

and whirligigs. Suddenly a noise
like gunshot, we stop and know,
immediately perceive the cracks that shoot

across the ice. Swift as swallows we retreat
skimming for the snowy shore
praying the ice will hold 'til we reach land.

Images of drowned faces upturned
like supplicants trapped below our feet,
haunt us back on solid ground.

The Stubble Field

A tawny fox stands exposed
in the same stubble field
that last year I walked through
as ears of wheat waved and lifted
waist-high about me. Leaving me
stranded half-woman, half swaying
wheat. He trots alert in the reaped
field that stretches vastly away,
sunlight sets the rough tufted stalks
a-sparkle, he turns flailing
at an imaginary crossroad
as if the shorn wheat still billowed
around him. He pauses, sniffs the air
adjusting to the slow accumulation of loss.

We gun the car down the empty early morning
road, tarmac not yet warmed up.
The fox with nowhere to hide shelters
in studied indifference, betrayed by the rise
of fur bristling at his neck. And I recall
pushing through the fluid wheat, ripping
sticky cobwebs from my bare knees,
unable to see my feet in the dense growth:
yet sensing something, some unease
lifting my hair at the nape. We speed by,
leaving the limitations and losses
of the landscape in the mirror
as the fox zig zags across the stippled
field and we all high tail it out of there.

Shadow

This lawn laid out in a large triangle is cooling your shadow like a sun dial
moving from noon to evening; you are all sheen and shade marking
time. Your image is a black silhouette on green grass. Whatever
angle you step out at in the garden your shadow side-steps you,
like a childs' puppet its strings stretched and taut. You sit on
the old swing, its seat mildewed and damp and pull
at the stout ropes until you move. Your shadow
stays swaying with you, swinging in the insistent
air that holds you in its outline as it pulls back
and forth, keeping time with you. You cannot
shake it off. Finally the sun retreats,
a pink glow brightens the horizon
until its light flattens and is gone
the shadow falls
you go indoors
alone.

The Mirror Demons

(from a poem by Adrienne Rich)

She watched herself
  noticed her reflection
    kept subtly changing.

Nothing sudden
  just an imperceptible
    drawing down

Of the lids of her eyes,
  the flesh of her lips.
    Sometimes, caught unaware

She wondered who
  that woman was,
    that woman

with no lover at her
  shoulder, jeered
    by the mirror demons.

II

My daughter and her mirror
  court each other daily
    mirrors love to flirt with youth,

it nibbles away at her
  feeds from her day by day
    and unnoticed takes more and more away.

She dances before it oblivious
  twisting and turning in its flattering light,
    it only reflects truth, at heart

it is pitiless and impervious
   to the grandeur of her self regard
      its tawdry tinsel light merely observes.

The mirror tells us how we see ourselves
   I want to warn my lovely daughter
      tell her of its jealousy and how it thieves.

III

Once I bathed in the quicksilver lake
   brushed out my yellow hair
      saw my reflection first thing

every morning, last thing at night.
   Now its searing vision threatens
      to undo me. Now I dread   .

Its lustre and stand unmasked
   before its crackled glaze.
      My image is brought sharply

into focus, I cringe from its unforgiving
   gaze, seeing only fragments,
      a mosaic of unremembered years,

I drown in its burnished sheen.
   Lift me like the blue/green iridescence
      in the speculum of a bird's wing.

IV

They need to look again
   these people who reflect in me
      blocking my ceiling sky.

All I do is take in the light
that hits me and bounce it back.
Like most, I have my demons,

but they are mine and I deal with them.
Other than an occasional silver sigh
I play dumb, like a good host

I try to be discrete, what am I supposed
to do? I am mercurial surely they can
appreciate I have my own truths to tell,

don't ask I say if you can't take it. I only repeat
what I see, nothing more nor less.
There is nothing in this for me.

Evening

We were surprised by the density
of the air, the way it oppressed our flesh,

how sunset bronzed the sky umber,
made the brittle light look rain glossed, Pulled

our skin taut while we fathomed the oncoming night;
the whole milky spume of the stars' light.

Bats are out, off flying almost following
the swallows flown home to roost.

Midges are still teeming in clouds,
the rooks clustered dark in the branches.

You mix an amphora of Mojitos, ice clinking
in the glass, sharp mint green as grass,

we sip and relax, let out long-held breath,
pull our chairs onto the deck.

Where we'll sit like flies caught in amber.
The midges vanish, the air thins,

we feel the first flecks of rain
spot on our skin.

A Loaded Gun

'For I have but the power to kill
without — the power — to die'.

EMILY DICKINSON

You opened the ribbed aluminium case
carefully in front of me. I thought it might
hold a camera, some lenses, but no,
packed in charcoal foam
a gun with a long narrow barrel
and some silver-tipped slugs;
I recoiled at the sight, the heft obvious
though we did not handle it,
tension sliced the air ripping ease
from the evening. Your husband
had left it, new, unused
menacing with intent.

The perfect O of the muzzle
was an all-seeing eye whose trajectory
seemed to target your canvases,
stacked against the wall as if in surrender.
In the crosshairs on an easel
the magenta and vermillion
of an unfinished painting
spilled like a ruptured bullseye.

We held the silver sarcophogus aloft,
you reached down to relieve me of its weight.
Gathering it in your arms you heaved it
up to the rafters. Now it is concealed
in your corrugated-roof studio.
You paint in its shadow, in its sights
all your images are disbursed.
Shot through with light and life.

A Measured Hour in the Menil Museum with Magritte

(Le Therapeute, 1967)

All the thousands of forgotten hours,
all the lonely afternoons, now spent; gone
into the deep blue/green patina
of forgetfulness, like seeing a fly
walking the inside of a window pane
seemingly held within a teardrop
while outside rivulets of rain descend.
In the Menil Museum a hatted
cast bronze man sits like Asclepius,
The Healer by Magritte;
at his feet his medicine bag, his cane.
Beneath the carapace of his cloak,
the barrel of his chest is exposed,
showing instead of ribs, a ribbed bird cage.
One bird fluttering inside where his heart
should beat, another perching outside, (on a rib perhaps?)
waiting to enter. The minutes we spent mulling
over Magritte's message are now obsolete,
as are the days he waited for the molten metal
to cool in its ceramic sarcophagus,
this is life lived in retreat. Moving always
away from that first moment when we sucked air,
joined together by the hasp of tied hours,
until the swell of our very last breath
and the condensation on the window recoils
curling away and Magritte tips his metal hat.

A Cow Observes Men

(after Carlos Drummond de Andrade)

We know how delicate they are, these humans,
but find them fastidious rather than noble.
They come to our pastures in machines
with huge wheels sometimes with bales of hay
borne aloft on mechanical horns.
They consult one another about the weather,
talk of the Beaufort scale, as if wind could be quantified.
We all know number five or six
when we feel it pelt our pinbone, hit our
dewlaps and watch white caps gathering
on the lake. But we know by now that they
don't listen when we low or bellow;
they call us Bos, Bo, Cow, Ox, call us what
you will; nothing changes, *know thyself.*
Our ancestors passed down tales of how,
in Roman times they fed us ivy,
Poet's Ivy for that matter.
We hated the stuff, it clogged our tongues
a beast would need a dozen stomachs to stomach it.
No, no José, you are the one without tradition
not us, we carry the world on our shoulders,
like Atlas we carry the globe of our heavy heads.
The world is not light; when your hands touch us
or your childrens' hands we feel our fate.
After your touch we tramp down to the bone beds
to chew on bones, craving the taste
of truth in the glow of phosphorus,
like we crave our own private belvedere.

Watching for the Comet

"...for the path of comets is the path of poets:
they burn without warning..."
    MARINA TSVETAEVA

Towards the west a small celestial trail
spirals the sky and nets me, Jubilant
stars in its wake so pinprick bright
I could trace them with my fingertips,
their old, cold light clusters like a chorus
chanting for the dead, all my kith and kin,
known and unknown tailing their light for me
to read in the night sky.
My head heavy like a newborn
as I stargaze. I see venus, earth's sister
and I see the lemon moon's
pale slice. Then I feel earth's grip
slip from me, I am unhitched, no longer bound,
I lose my bearing in a sea of fiery stars.
Floating in the firmament I have become
an adumbrated body of falling light.

Photograph: The Arvon Foundation

JEAN O'BRIEN is a Dubliner now living in the Irish Midlands. She has published three previous collections: *The Shadow Keeper* (Salmon, 1997), *Dangerous Dresses* (Bradshaw Books, 2005) and *Lovely Legs* (Salmon 2009). She has an M.Phil in Creative Writing from Trinity College, Dublin. She facilitates creative writing classes for a wide variety of organizations from the Irish Writers' Centre, Dublin City Council and various County Council to Mountjoy, Limerick and the Midlands Prisons. She was Writer-in-Residence for Co. Laois. Her work is broadcast on RTE Radio, Sunday Miscellany and elsewhere. She did a collaboration with the artist Ray Murphy on an interpretation of her winning poem Merman which was held in The Arthouse, Stradbally. She was the 2008 recipient of the Fish International Poetry Award and in 2010 she won the biennial Arvon International Poetry Award.